An English Anthology

An English Anthology

Leonard Nolens

translated by
Paul Vincent

CARCANET

C Λ R C Λ N E T

First published in Great Britain in 2018 by
Carcanet
Alliance House, 30 Cross Street
Manchester M2 7AQ
www.carcanet.co.uk

A CIP catalogue record for this book is
available from the British Library,
ISBN 978 1 78410 574 7

Book design: Andrew Latimer
Printed in Great Britain by SRP Ltd., Exeter, Devon

The publisher acknowledges financial
assistance from Arts Council England.

Contents

FROM Sung to Exhaustion and Dated

I'm no longer a son or a seer.
My parents I know only
   as a semanteme looked up by chance.
The places where they lie together
   out of the wind, north-eastwards from my hand
I have marked on this map in red
   like a dreamer who never sets out.

I'm no longer a man or a lover.
The metastasis of the first word
   has infected it all, the limp sex
   lies rolled up somewhere in the dusty folds
   of my voice, the tears came
   seldom, welled up as a natural urge
   for which there's no room.

I'm no longer a poet or a figment
   of what once kept us apart.
The metaphors I've built around us
   collapse like an uninhabitable room
   in which my eyes and my fists fall open
   in the clarity of the last day.

Not to be able to write another poem
off the cuff.
Not a poem like a person
with its hand on its heart, a man
who stands, exists
in the crowd, understands
the crowd, means, yes
means
with his heart in his hand
what he says.

Not to be able to write another poem
except with a hundred fingers at once
increasing hand over hand
in ineffability.

Not a poem save with a mouth
that is sung tight
in a mouth in
a mouth in
a mouth.

Not a poem save with an eye
that every second changes
its face.

I waited and none of you came.
I was silent as if murdered,
but even a corpse is an eloquent proof
of our feverish lot.

No one was waiting for me.
For years I shouted you out
like pain, like bad food, like music.
I was your numeral, naming at times,
a trembling hand that leafs through your mouths,
I became silence, silence that falls
between wars, underwear and glasses, falls
between you and me.

I have danced for everyone, almightily
still almost in the drum of my skin.
But no one struck,
struck up and made me sound.

I remain the child
that's born each morning grumbling
after your wrangling in clammy sheets
and a careless alphabet.

I, Poet, carilloneur
with the out-of-date fingering
in the churning of the hands suspended
as a divining rod, weathervane, crowing
mene tekel in instalments of my body
that has danced up against death –

nailed to the sky,
powdered with Great Bear, ram seed, earth wind,
I live in the hectic brain of this century
like a lost lobe, a mental fault,
a deceptive expression of the eternal now.

Right through the cobwebs
of tricky politics and fermenting cultures
I make the conceited horoscope, selfish
at night within exciting belts of speech
unbuckled.

I am your dropped stitch,
your internal bruising
after the genuflection to mammoth mammon
and Nirwana nowhere.

I am the manhole of silence.

FROM **Paul Celan**

Today autumn comes and eats
out of your hand.
Travel-weary it drapes itself,
too late, a cruel friend,
over you. Its hair tousled
and its limbs wind and slowly gold
shamelessly begin the marriage
you've awaited so long.

Now it eats out of your hand.
It eats the hand
that your voice once dated
to infinity, eats, eats your eye
that saw deeper, deeper than
the current of the Seine,
of time.

Autumn, it eats
itself away in you.

What's left is the garb
of icy lace and snow
in which your voice shrouds itself, cries
wounded and preserved, deeper
than the current of the Seine,
of time.

Invented nothing. Nothing.

Only your voice
broadcast, your breath
vertically mapped,
your words alibis
to calm silences.

Said yourself to pieces.
Your land a bushel of ground,
some snatches of crooning, verbs, produced
with a time-resistant tongue,
with artificial light, hard
spit, strong
as the rock...

Gave air
to the released
flame —

trace
that confirms
your absence.

Washed away.
Scream sediment.
Heart no longer subject
to high and low tide.
Hunger sicked up as a surfeit.
A long voice your life, long fall,
a cadence painfully studied like
a diver draws his body and gives it
to greedily drinking water, drunk on eternity –

upstream through the streets
always your steps conflicting with light,
untangling light in your word
your own glittering spun
in a slummy quarter of the world.
And yourself custodially released
like a spider guards, inhabits
its splendid trace, lives on choking
after its death, and singing cobweb
that is ravelled
from mouth to mouth,

a ritual
for heretics.

You could go nowhere
without the dull sound of porcelain
with which you were addressed
reopening the wound of the alphabet
reduced to nine letters
of your name, your name the unwanted beginning
of each poem.

That name was not Celan.
That name was Jew, Jew, a word
palmed off on you
like a birthmark,
a long-drawn-out curse,
a flight into the provisional book
from which your brothers came,
Job and Jeremiah and Isaiah.

It's you
who read me, light years hence
your knees pulled up
against this autumn, against
this poem.

Your lips fill up
with loss.
Your head, heavy
impossible thing,
has rolled from your elbow behind
the twilight, overexposed
your heart
as soon as your cry
lost
its mouth.

At last you've been
indiscreet.

In Memoriam Matris

This hundred-year-old house
neither the swearing
nor this eternal house
can take pity on
your grimaces.

This house, oh
the calvary, the room
intended for guests,
the room, you, the room you
whom I now enter, no
no no, oh
you stink my girl,
my girl my flower,
my rotting flower,
my flower my flower.

And no one keeps your gift intact, stops
this giving, again
(the first scream)
and again
you gave us away
and exposed us to the season
that colours surging mirrors
over your face
cancer, this moaning
that says you beyond the stone
under which you lie blurred.

I still have to learn you.

The book you've become
takes up all my years
and my eyes.

You make me
see black.

In vain I follow the pagination
from the tomb to the fraction
that counted us out
from woman to man.

I still have to read me.

FROM **Proteus**

Belief

At home at table I've seen forests move, heard estates
and people change names.
In that round number on the tongue lay the power to change
    villages
in a trice.
In those secrets I was gradually initiated.
Gold was denied me.
And that denial I cash in here and transfer it to many.

I've lived hidden and quiet as a running tab in the hands of
the landlord.
And in gossip and melons I was proscribed
by the grocer.
Did they know I was being traded over the counter?

And with that growing silence my longing grew to go
poste-restante in every town,to teach all proletarians
to play the piano and usurp the name of the king.
I want all his winged adjutants to make love to their gruff
    recruits.
I want the queen to yield her sex to the errand boy.
Let us take another turn,
Let that earth rotate on the tip of your tongue and snap it up,
Just trip over your tongue in towns and commonplaces.
Let us swop laments and scarcity for magnanimous Dutch:

We are no longer that dissolution of factors and family
and the Lower House,
We are no longer the eternal deficit in the balance of payments
    of speech.

For I believe in this book,
I believe in the book that comes to blows with its reader,
The book that like an old clock is a day ahead of the hand
    that
absent-mindedly wound it.
I believe in the book that strips us leaf by leaf and leaves
nothing in us but growth principles.
I believe in the book that makes us thin with pain.
I believe in the book that makes us fat with hunger.

No one has yet spoken his short breath,
No one has yet turned his burning joints outward,
No one has yet rewritten his wild rhythms as ritual.

I believe in this book as in the present non-existent.

New Land

Each day breakfast with incantations and much sun at
    table.
And thick newspapers like a lucid theorem
For workdays shorter than a cry of lust.
Lunch never comes to an end.
We speak smoothly to each other as if we were drinking
And in my hand your head, heavy as a holdall.
Everyone's forever calling on us.
Playfully the body is exchanged.
We give our seed to old women and passers-by…

… New Land, wait for us until we're cured,
Wait, lost lanes full of petal shades, wait until our
burning soles lose themselves in you,
Waiting, my park declared dead with all your portamento
    of countless
green and quails,
Wait, luminous ponds full of gurnard and eager mortals,
Wait, breakfast with fruitful conversations,
With paradise grains in our charred hands
And with the garish colours of the dawn
And with our solid sex like alms under the table
And with wise friends and girlfriends, talking of fucking,
And with those devilish snatches of memory of a right
    family,
Wait, telluric laugh, caught deep in the nut's cheek, wait
Till they come to redeem you, wait
Till we're cured.

FROM Anonymous

Undercurrent

I've no powerful feeling for life, chest puffed out.
I've no splendid emotional life to lavish
Or sick spots which are supposed to make my self more popular
With weepy people and the public purse.
I'm not an intellectual who always waffles
With someone else's lukewarm chops, has never saved up a few
    words
In his own blood and spit.

But I do have a good and strong character.
I have an earthy character in which the sowing breath
Of another can take root and blossoms
Up to my throat that is warm and moist with love
For the word and its soundless mental leap.
Thus not I but everything in my hands gains its face.
I'm a maternal undercurrent and make world of everything.

Tuesday Morning 12 October 1978, Six-thirty in De Pelikaan

My pub is emptying. The city's filling up.
I see suits and overalls leaving their homes.
I don't get what will and what wheel
Possesses you every day to drive those difficult machines
With a childlike hand
And add up all those figures with a dreamy look.

And you, my resting, my rusting poet friends,
Calvinists have gagged and unmanned your throats,
You don't talk, no, you just toss something off,
You wind up most sublime mechanisms
With an educated right hand – it's right in every way!
Yet it's not right at all, your heart.

My tongue is caught between the hands at half past six.
I can see my death sitting peering in the hubbub
Of smart stains on floor tiles or a skinned lower lip,
In this descent of my voice soon sleeping lost
Among empty bottles and the soft arm of one absent,
This red pencil rolled away in unwritten letters.

I should like to be yours, the people's
And pull the day like a sack over my head.

Prologue

I've nothing more. I'm nothing more.
My book is a mess from the start.
And I who wanted to make reality.

I want to wake at last from your social graces of me.
I want to recover at last from my ancient history in you.

But my existence has been confiscated.
My tongue grows old. I'm on my way.
And there's nothing to get closer to.

I'm still a separate manifestation of you.
And I still have a body of my own since you.
I want my personal story.

But I have no secret. I am a secret.
And I who wanted to make reality.

All this said with the leather hand.

I

You're already included in my start.
In you I began, in your ever-changing forms
I was half given, your elusive essence
Is written in my body for a lifetime.
You don't leave me. You never leave me in peace.
In you I find my freedom, my compulsion.

You are the restless place where I don't yet exist.
You are the hour that must fill all my cracks
With thinking singing, the most impractical being.
You are the sign plaited into my guts
And you're what I must become, one day a perfect likeness.

You're the trip that forbids me the trip, the hunger
That eats me and may satisfy me. You are.
You are and you are not. You bring me to light
If you want. And to your capriciousness, your structures
And strictures I'm committed and consigned.
But I can't visit you, name you, possess you.

What I mean today I always owe to you.
You keep me upright above all nights in those cycles
Of gullible creature, of world becoming useless.
You say, I just have all and nothing in common with you.

I bear you in my head and don't know you.
You bear me in your womb and wait for my appearance.
Perhaps I'll be a still-born child.

Iowa City 2

Here it's night. With you it's day. I look at you.
I hear desire trying out its weird instruments
Beneath a moon of ivory. I hear a very old sobbing
Of the air as our letters cross noiselessly
Above the splashing blue, the sparkling deep that I know
From your eyes, my sweet, for with you it's day, for good.

When I dream of you painfully soft patches
Run through my body. When I write to you I go all hard
Down there, a sing-song thinking opens and goes on
In my chest, I grow high, broad, a fragrant tree
Of sleepless music, my sweet, for with you it's light
For good. I go to the window. I see myself looking at you.

FROM Exile

Traitor

With exorbitant muddy feet, the conservative-minded blush
Of a bourgeois past in the countryside,
With hysterical hunger for study I came for sun, for sense,
For outrageous beauty among the city folk.
With cheek, with ethical sense from the Christian school,
With a heathen need for myself, with a holy thirst
For musical metaphysics that, crystal clear, determine my place
Among the people and the four elements, so I came
For bread, for birth and death among the city folk.

I moved into a flat in the lonely bustle
Of a street without end. In pubs and libraries
I sought and found the friends with whom I shared myself,
My money, my insomnia and my green poems.
We put our books in a pile, with young earnestness
And egotism we sat in state like princes among princes
At that high, strong, self-made table of the word.
But one of us wanted to be king and went.

Narcissus

It's so hard to love
The things you make –
You look with endearment at a hand
Full of chaff and corn
And you bake your bread wrongly;
You weld with tinkering eyes,
With a heart full of active emotion
Two left-hand sides together.

Yes, it's difficult, just difficult
And beautiful to touch yourself, today
And also finally, it is difficult
And beautiful to regain yourself tomorrow
In the things that you make.
Sometimes you'd accept a death in return.

Slave Girl

My reality speaks seven languages
And often has little or nothing to say.
It lives like someone waiting to convert
And not knowing to whom or what.

My reality has a strong feeling
For light that is not there.
My reality has lots of knowledge
Of things that escape it daily.
Absence is its most natural heart.

My reality is a black slave girl
At the feet of invisible masters.

Week

Like a beast I go round sniffing at my days.
I turn around them wagging my tail, snuffle them, I root
    them up
Sniffing with my hot, steaming snout of inquisitive dog.
I eat some. I piss on them. I toss them aside.

Monday reeks of the classic Sunday consternation
Of footballer's grief and tiresome piano lessons in D major,
Of existential whiffs of sperm, quizz questions and meringue.

Tuesday's already tiring, Tuesday begs for the strength
To foreswear this saintly life of a wastrel,
To serve someone with the breathtaking aspirations of the
    upstart.

Wednesday hates the hot smell of sweets of its public parks.
Mittwoch wants grown-up afternoons full of planetary culture.
Wednesday fathers bequeath sharp intellects to their idiotic
    family.

Thursday goes gloomily to the whores, sticks
His pathetic thing into the personalities of merciful women.
Thursday goes early to bed to shorten its conscious hours.

Friday sits with friends on terraces downtown
Or writes home for money, for comfort, for the sake of writing,
    for nothing.
Friday evening, fish among the hours, parties or hangs itself.

Saturday is room to once again creatively wash out your navel,
To count your coins under the wet skirt of moved mothers.
Saturday is me, or out of boredom makes a few more kids.

Exile

It is not something, it is not someone
Who yesterday left you perhaps.
It is not something or someone who abandoned you
to your fate here today.

It is life itself, this light
With its so insubstantial face.
It is the right placelessness
Of your body put on a stool here.

It is the sky, a flight of clouds
On the retina of a blind man, it is
Endless this lasting for want
Of breath divided into measures and times.

It is life itself, this trembling
That has you, this weaving that you are.
It is life itself that today
Leaves you alone with your specific gravity.

It is today with dreadful weather and human flesh
An eternal flu of the soul, your beast.
It is nothing but life itself that has here
Consigned you to your fate today.

L*

Fate's lottery brought us slowly together.
Passion was a school for patience,
A flame in the dreaming knot of the tongue.

You slept in your name until I came and said it.

What then began is still beginning, the journey –
Till suddenly fate's lottery pulled us apart.
We're alone now, but each other's.

L**

You're the only one who's eavesdropped on my life in concrete
time, within earshot, in the halfway house.
There we separate in the mornings to think up stories during
    the day
that bring us together in the evenings by the blue kitchen fire.
The silent bustle of the light that passed into us is calmly
    reduced
to silence with cooking and talking.

The round table is the right word to sit at and eat of
each other so that you grow in me and I in you.
The night is clear as the short orgasm that we have slowly
    learned together
over the years.
Afterwards we separate gain to devise each other for
the evening and night.

So our days are made of useful loneliness.

FROM The Enduring Departure

Place and Date

I was born in Belgium, I'm Belgian.
But Belgium was never born in me.

I was born in Flanders forever,
But Flanders wasn't where my oldest cradle stood.

Flanders is my modern artificial mother now
From who I did not acquire my child's tongue,
Whose heartbreaking gabble I study.
Flanders slowly became my historical father
Whose ancestors are not mine.

I was born in Limburg, cold,
A cold, cold province.
I got hot there.

I was also born in Bree, of Loon
And Liège, a ghost town, a middle class
With a sing-song whiny twang
That dreams me aloud when I sleep,
When sleeping I'm immersed
In slow Low German.
                    That is music
Which is older, more familiar than this
And which I'm trying to transpose here.

And finally, as the healthy son
Of much cannon fodder, finally
I was born in 1947,
A raw date, a hopeful time,
A worldwide shortage that grows
In me, in me becomes grown-up.

The Enduring Departure

You're always the man who asks questions and listens.
You've no other input than your attention.
You question the silence. You pick the emptiness clean,
Its monotony, its metronome, its mother beat
That for twenty years you've tried to imitate.

Was that freedom, then, to imprison you here?
As if a man can decide anything in his dreams!
As if they were there, different rooms, means, ways
In wine, cynicism, travel. No, here was the courageous flight,
The cowardly house full of self-confident loneliness.

And here, with the strict pathos of your childhood,
You slowly became a scholar with no special field,
A faithful lover without a lover, a priest
Without God, perhaps a seed that travels the whole desert
And time, yours, this one, a hectic lesson in patience.

And here, where you read the Tao with your wrong eyes
Of the West, and the Torah that cannot give birth to you,
And where you look for music like Bach
Can explain the heartbeat of your brain function,here
You can't leave, you must interrogate the white, question
The sheet, begin each day with the end of your dream.

Here is your house and the going. Here's your enduring
    departure.

Verklärte Nacht

We sit naked at table. Your eyes light up the room.
Your phosphorescent butterfly hands rearrange the air
When you talk to me or sleep on the black tablecloth.

I touch them daily. Their lifeline knows my name.
Their transparent arteries hide the course of my fate,
    the flight
Of our blood that changes the white of your cheeks into
    flecked desire.

The french window blows open. The start of rain rustles
    through the trees,
Sprinkles the tugging window in which you sit shining,
Light in which I see myself, in whom I perhaps disappear.

You pile the plates, remove the crumbs and pour some
    more wine.
In the kitchen I hear the blue porcelain and the knives
    clinking,
Far off. My legs hurt from not being able to come to you.

Fright

It's so brittle,
It's so awkward having you close to me.
You're living here just like that and suddenly,
You're living here now and right up
against me, with the snow
Of your face, the bloodstain
Of your mouth and your sex.
With all your warm weight you lean
On my life.
With the peering pain
Of your past's clarity,
The cold, electric blue
Of your eyes, so awkwardly fragile.

I see you go through the rooms,
It's my own life that has made itself beautiful and is
    walking there.
It's my years that pick up a book,
that shift dark things with elegant hands.
It's my time that still walks there on thin ankles.
It's my morning that stands there
In the high, wide doorway,
My short duration in its whitest manifestation.

It's today with golden hair,
With big musical ears.

A Natural Street

The garden fills with snow. There is great music here
Of kissing butterflies, deep from the heights of nowhere.

The grass and the hedges stand in their singing colourlessness
Vanishing, paths discover their own life melodies there

In this soft hard white.   A blowing begins so spare
That the eye listens to, a hand spreading signs without distress

In the air's empty history. This sows slight seeds of fear
Of fleeting winging in silky-winged ones: a moment,
     a moment there

In the windows huge curtains open, the moon appears
As the watching ear of the choir director, the flow of song

From above falls silent in the grass, the hedges, the paths
     henceforth where
Everything becomes almost a nothing of dazzling openness.

FROM Tributary

Deontology

How far can I go, how far in solitude, how deep,
And without soon disappearing from her sight?
She, whom I have absorbed into me, the one worthy of mention
On whom I live, of whom I must die, how far
Can she follow me, the blackest path, the narrowest road,
The law prescribed for her by my birth?

She is the one I steal from in every way.
I am the the ghost that haunts her, that must taste
The poisoned honey of her blood to became healthy,
Daily I suck her to death. – How long can she take this?
How scared is she, absorbed in this solitude, how small?
Till, while alive, we've disappeared from each other's sight?

Tributary

She sleeps and all is still. Then it snows in the rooms
Of the house that I inhabit with my lover.
She lies there nude and white, a breathing piece of stone,
A large and awkward statue that I must bump into,
A sharp-edged weight that I must carry every day,
Every night that her sleep keeps me from sleep.

I am alone with her. Alone with her I come
Walking down the years, for her name points me the way
And in her eyes I see my blind time mirrored.
She lies there nude and white, a breathing piece of stone,
On which I've whetted all my blunt existence
And still whet, even when I sleep and, shouting, dream of her.

High Fever

Someone brought up by God breaks his bread
In a different time, he tastes the raw food of Jesus
In every form of life: all stings because it shines,
Because it reflects the more thorough work and being,
Shadow under which an unborn child chokes in its sleep.
Someone poisoned by God won't ever come right.

You too, who've not believed since you were twenty,
Day by day you still must eat of that hunger
For perfection, you must drink of that thirst
For what's not yet existing. Yes, he is dead,
But the stomach where his blood once boiled
And the tongue too, the mouth with which he was thought,
They've never been cured of their high fever.

Poor devil that you are, still searching
For gruff holiness that strikes on the rock of the world,
That spits in the hard face of emptiness, baseness.
You, who were brought forth by God, who lost him,
You'll never escape that origin, you hate the seed
That in you now cries out for a big family, tomorrow.

Sunday

You've had a hard time being alone all day.
Eaten an egg, stared busily out of the window
And drunk coffee, read the latest woes
And thought hard about your future of today.
The things a person can take.

If you go out this evening, don't forget
To take off your grave face at the front door.
The street doesn't like grave faces.
And don't forget your sunglasses – that dreamy look
Can cost you your life these days.
And leave your penknife, leave your cash at home,
You might bump into someone, for instance
A man who's had a hard time being alone all day,
A gorgeous girl who talks hoarsely of love,
A brat who yaps he's your son and wants dough.

No, stay indoors. Stay alone
With your guilty slowness and bottles,
Your crooked page, your mirror where you see no one,
Your time that has no time or tidings.
Just stay alone with this holy word of Sunday.
You bang and stamp on it.
And every letter sounds hollow.

Paranoia

They say poets should keep their tongues in check.
They, that's the fashionable journalists who squat my clothes
And tomorrow wear my designs. They are the head cooks
Who sup on my meat and spit in my pans.
They are the weedkillers and dead doctors of poetry.
But who has clothed the naked, fed the hungry?

No, my canny old tongue of yours is also mine
And what it does is simply often pathetically conceived.
Your metric sports jackets and rhyme trousers I'll keep well
    clear of.
Your insipid sonnet snaps, no, I'm sorry, thanks.

I can't help it, the most sublime prosody
Comes from the gut, finally each soul thinks intestinally.
(It's different with my Capital Letter, here it comes:
It is the G key of my awkward staves.)

This charms or astonishes perhaps. It wasn't meant like that.
Much in these lines has been knocked together with hate
    and anger,
Even with good intentions my road goes straight to hell.
Sufferers go to hell, there is no merit in pain.

Words, seeds and cents were made to roll.
Never put them in the bank book of the obvious form.
The most intimate form is the man's rhythm: poetry
With balls then, as Pavese said, and he swallowed his death.

FROM **Melancholy**

Playing the Beast

The squinting otter that sees much further than me,
With its sparkling webbed feet,
with its webbed feet sparkling
With salt crystals it floats up
On its back, it holds the mighty mystery
Of the mussel in its hand, it smashes
The black mould on the pebble it's fished
And slurps the night-time innards of my origin.

The orang-utan that walks into my dreams
With its sleepy gait, the deep seriousness
Of all its splendid manners,
With its utterly calm hands,
With its hands utterly calm
From thinking it measures and breaks reeds and sticks
The probing point in the ground, sounds out
The anthill, the swarming ground
Of my existence, and catches the good sweetness.

And I, who've looked at those two
With my fumbling hands,
With my hands fumbling
From thinking, remembering, reconsidering
What is man's lot, boredom, debts, drink,
Noise, migraine, war, I and my hands
Found nothing better to do today
Than to imitate
These cool, calm and collected hands, these bloodthirsty
    webbed feet.

Minimum Wage

Today it's not the truth I seek,
No Nazarene fisherman to rob me of my death,
No Viennese doctor to give my penis elecution lessons,
No Trier philosopher who has my mandate at the bank.

Today it's not goodness that I seek,
No Gandhi, bald and skinny, word right to the bone,
And no Thérèse de Lisieux. (What was it the little one said?
'I must feel You hard, otherwise there's chaos,
Hard and exhausting, or I shan't be at rest.')

No goodness, no, dammit, I know what goodness is.
Goodness is a stinking bed, a girl's voice
Aged sixty, a gobbing wad of flesh
In formaldehyde pillows, a trembling mouse's paw
Which I once ate and which I still don't like.

Today it's not beauty that I seek.
Beauty speaks for itself when I open my hands
In the ivory of my favourite chord, seven fingers,
A minor, from the nocturnes of Chopin,
That consumptive at his Pleyel in Nohant.

No, the true and the good and the beautiful today are
A living for engineers, therapists and artists.
But I, I'm a poet.
And on my humble chair, with my craftsman's pride
I seek a solid, proper and elegant way
Here, today, in this time, to survive.

It

It comes in the morning, the alarm stops and the news has
    been ordered.
The foaming cheeks, the razor, the eyes, they hang tin-plated
In the mirror, a slow syrup of buzzing escapes from taps
and holes, and the clock face and its hands look idly on.

It comes at lunchtime, the meat has been carved,
    the summer is high
In the bottles that pass round and tremble, no salt can stop
    the bleeding,
The glasses start screaming and silently shatter in pieces,
    blinded
By a zenith, and pets, guests melt into a single face.

It comes in the evening, it likes to come best in the evening,
    the nights.
The ancient spittle freezes on the tongue of the kisser,
    the stroking
Paralyses the stroked one, her dreams depict a dreamless
    sleep
In the iron bed of an icy hotel, but *wake* me now, *wake* me.

It is a healthy exhaustion from before and after this life,
Which simply won't forget us, it's a kind of pressing rest
Which relaxes the muscles and painfully forces the forehead
    onto the edge
Of the table, a bottomless wish to sink into someone,
    something.

FROM Love's Declarations

Craw

She stands at the window staring
Down and points to the people,
She says it again and again:
Life is nothing, is nothing.

Just hear how cajoling that sounds
When she listens and groans, with that lust;
Life is nothing, is nothing.

It swells from her mouth, a hymn
To our futility, she puts death
For me in a clear light,
Life is nothing, is nothing.

And I go, I pick her up again
From those depths and bear her to bed
And press close to her again.

I jerk her face towards me
And lick and swallow all her tears.
I eat the craw so greedily
From her throat that she sobs deep in me.

FROM Etiquette

Door

How long, dawdling like a skinflint
Who counts his change prior to the journey,

How long have I stood here knocking
At the door of life,

With the bashfulness of women
Who're ashamed of their beauty,

With my hunger not spotting
The hangover after the meal, how long

Have I stood here knocking
At the door of life,

With teenage pique that spat
In the safes of my parents' house,

Spoiled by being unborn
In the sun of mother's belly, how long,

With the misplaced courtesy
Of an unhappy person, how long

Have I stood here knocking
At the door of life,

Which was open.

October Sun

I live small here, hidden, in a wooden house
And live across the whole width of the wood
As far as a pain where my reason can go no further.

I also play under the trees with my absent ones,
Burn in peace there my slow blood among the flowers
And hide my Bovarysm in October.

I live small here at the level of my poems
And to the rhythm of a love that exists
Because she's Leen and mine and not private.

I need that gold of her absence here
And soon will pour it out over us, we are not poor.
From a reliable source I've heard we're both here.

Children

My Most Solid House

My most solid house anchored yonder
In the heart of a provincial town, a bay
Edged with lime-trees and a church, a ring
Of white gables and a monastic school
Where boys stood singing in clipped Latin.
Through bare classrooms rustled Greek whispers
Of men in black. And this is their lesson.

This solid house was entirely made
Of beggars and tramps who thronged the doors,
Who sat round the table baking thick hosts
For Christmas and Easter so as to be born later.
This solid house was entirely made
Of open windows and hoarse Gregorian.

That house was also a long, deep dialogue
Of two pianos, a furious blazing row
Of four women's hands in the clear ground floor,
A dark fight that moulded the dreams
Of a boy in his floating attic.

I sleep there with the girl's heart of friends.
The little penis of my love paints
The sheets and the future with tepid roses.
I scream what later I'll do slowly.

I dream there ad nauseam of my life
And live there ad nauseam on my dreams.
And on my knees I creep toward you.

Class Reunion

Forty-somethings, drink and stories. Smoker's throats scraping
Like skating half the night over the full moon
On Reppel pond. And then guffawing in a gang
To an abandoned farm of snow and muck.

Sixteen and the resilience of flick knives, muscles.
The fist-thick padlock creaked like pack ice breaking up.
Knocking back the bolts clanged against the dome
Of freezing air, and went on spinning through the village heart.

We dragged the crates hurrahing from the stalls
And the beer was thick and sharp like the mother's milk
We spoke there with steaming mouths.
Maurits struck up the Salve Regina and jerked off.

He spurted as we sang and the sweethearts slept
In satin rooms yonder under oppressive roofs.
Cigarettes went round. We lay in the white
Blowing at the stars and all out of stories.

Between Five and Seven

Between five and seven pm
When nothing happens,
The mercury rises in all who are sick
And the children learn to swear.
Singing and cursing they fling the milk
Off the table, stamping they hold
Their hunger up like their most precious toy
Between five and seven pm
When nothing happens.

Then people let their bodies sink
Into trams and kitchens, into pubs
And into thoughts too, they raise their arms
To heaven and hold their suspect papers
Up to the light, and between their hands
The rolling headlines stretch,
Soldiers and fires run from left
To right, and newspapers and tears
Can no longer be kept apart.

Between five and seven pm
When nothing happens, here
In my local, 'The Quiet Rain'.
Meanwhile everything is carefully
And silently taken outside,
The grand piano and the piebald tomcat,
The severe flutes and the table silver,
The grandfather clock and the guttering chandelier
And in lacquered coffins Mum and Dad.

Weariness

When we, the grown ups, are tired
Of talking to each other,
When we're tired of sleeping
With each other, walking
And doing business with each other,
Dining and warring

With each other, when we're so tired
Of each other, of othering
each other, we put the cat
On our shoulder, go into the garden
And look for the children's voices behind
The high hedges and in the tree house.

And silently we lay our weariness
In the grass, and the years that slept
Heavy and dark in the hem
Of our coat bare themselves up there
In a boy's throat and dance up
And down in a girl's moist mouth.

When we, the grown ups, are tired
Of talking,
Of talking,
Of talking to each other,
We go into the garden and silence ourselves
In the cat, in the grass, in the child.

Late

Slow.
Slow.
Slow your step.

Step slower than your heartbeat wants.

Slow down.
Slow down.
Slow down your longing

And vanish in moderation.

Don't take your time
And let time take you –
Late.

Alice

Slept, long and deep, in black.
Our light was outside all night.
My blond light-hearted one hurries half-naked
And fused with her swirling skirt
Through the room, hips swaying
And whistling she combs the light, the thick light
Of her frizzy hair and the morning.

The sun loves to play with her breasts
And leaps on her back, splashes
Her neck and her shoulders, she stands there
Simmering deep in the heart
Of the mirror and grabs me there
With her look: come with me now, come with me.
I vanish in a gold cloud of slivers.

Always Tomorrow was the Journey

The Busker

The fat man's there again. My wife hangs over the sill
To watch his clambering baritone.
His head voice is the local house painter
And the town's savings swell in his squeeze box.
Oh, every day he elects himself mayor
Of our hearts, his career makes me green as hell.

He has earned his own hard money singing.
No one can resist his throat, his gullet.
His big mouth is daily bread, his whole life
Is a basket of songs that's woven wherever he goes.
His hunger is a long street strewn with coins.

Men slow their steps. Their listening bakes his bread.
With their delight he'll buy some summer trousers today.
My wife is quiet. He climbs slowly till he's naked
In her hearing, and his absence will never go away.
A girl lifts up her skirt and tapdances to my text.

Easter Letter

I've got to tell you, I'm sitting here alone.
The day before yesterday I turned fifty-one in the rain
At a quarter to nine in the morning, I'd completely forgotten.
Got as presents two pairs of black socks and Portnoy's
Delights*, plus three summer shirts and fugues by Bach.
Yesterday, Easter, my sons came to dinner in Berchem,
Cream of tomato soup, leg of lamb, passion fruit ice cream.
Jonas is going to build tree houses and watch game in Congo,
David's writing a story in which I don't know his father
And Adriaan's selling his truck, no more Marrakesh.
Today Driekoningenstraat is full of Moroccans.
Tomorrow Leen goes back to the museum, she's fifty-one too.

Those are the facts, no, the thoughts, no,the feelings
Of which I'm made on this still wet Easter Monday.
Those are the people who've laid their eggs
In this unfindable nest of tobacco fug and messy papers.
I sit on it and brood, I don't know what will come of it.
I love them all and still am a man alone.
I drink my coffee, take my pills, thrust my hands
Deep into words in search of more family.
Beyond the closed curtains the supposed streets
Go their way to the harbour, in the east wind I hear the trains
And stay. And through my room run the tracks and points
That I can't see. The fug! The messy papers!

*A reference to a collection of essays, Genietingen (1998), by Ethel Portnoy
  (1927–2004).

Blooming

What nonsense is that, putting
Your life at risk?
Why? For what? For who?

Someone in you, a dog
Thrown out of a moving car
In July on the way to the South,

Someone in you, a minister
Full of remorse and millions
In a foreign account,

Someone in you, a rose bush
With blossom pain
Just before the axe,

Someone in you, a child
From Year 1, a boy
Who didn't want his birth, someone

In you couldn't bark something,
Couldn't confess something,
Couldn't bloom something, someone in you
Couldn't love his parents.

What nonsense is that, putting
Your life at risk?
Why? For what? For who?

Barking.
Confessing.
Blooming.
Loving.

FROM **Kicking Foetus**

Tristitia

There was a time I believed in my time.
A man, a day, a woman would enter
The room and understand my bed,
Stroke my sleeplessness with a giant tongue,
Raise my dwarf heart to the height of a sentence.
But two who made me there went violently to sleep
And slept on. They slept and sleep far into my day.

Their gambler's blood is my tristitia.

There came a time when I felt chilled by the breeze
That played in the morning through the blue curtains
Of the boy's room. I lay in that empty music
Waiting for my life, for my own life.
I waited there and shared that waiting with no one.
And no one was that travelling landscape of the sea,
That unborn person whose photo I studied.

Clan

There was a time I lived in a snow-white house
With dozens of doors. And no door would shut,
We were the keys. And in the mother room
A round table stood like an open book
Reading itself as we spoke, as we ate
Each other. That was an outspoken time.

On Sundays the wine sang itself up there
Into bottles and throats. Snuffed honey candles
Leaked their wax in embroidered bastard coats-of-arms.
There was no world outside the partying clan.
No one could interrupt our blood, and always,
Always a table was set for total strangers.

White Bread

In the cellars the cakes and cheeses wheeled their aromas
Upwards, empty-stomached we went dizzily to mass.
And there sat Jesus bottled up in his monstrance.

He starves us with the red-hot white of his bread.
O Lord, I am not worthy for you to come to me,
But speak just one word and I shall become well.

And after that starter your nutritious virginity,
My Dina, my Dina, the white pleats of your apron
Stretched over your tummy. Oh inconvenient democracy!

My glass table bell sings the praises of our dead staff.
Hand me that roast game from forty years ago
While your bosom strokes my boy's cheeks.

Lout

There was a time when in the small cup of my hands
The blue and red and green of the marbles chinked
Against each other, the whole rainbow of my winnings.

I put it in my pillowslip, I slept on it,
And all the louts in town dreamed of my treasure.
That's how it would be. That's how my future stretched out.

I've still not forgotten that rainbow, still
I'm the greedy capitalist of all my dreams.
In my head the marbles go on angrily chinking.

I'm still the roughest gambler in the Vrijthof
And my pretention knows no bounds further afield.
I'm a winner, and only the winner can share.

Archaic

The gold swivel-arse of the tower cock
Has tired of dancing and bled to death and lays
Its phoney egg, there, that setting sun.

Below the last lads play with marbles
In the round square, they shove the leathers
From their knuckles and count the gleaming take.

Women boom buckwheat pancakes
Across the Vrijthof, great hunger hastens
With black hands towards the table linen.

He crosses himself and spreads the Liège syrup
Over Mum's pancakes with bacon, carafes
Of apple juice go silently from hand to hand.

Cats snatch crackling from the plates.
Parents feed the family's remnants
Like squabbling sparrows in the courtyard.

The brothers and sisters lay their Latin
And Greek on the table, drop off together
Over sums. The cock has gone to the moon.

The Clock Strikes

There was a time when a father hit me
With his time, the striking of two fists.
He was made of that beyond his will.

I see a short and broadly built sorrow
That sang Schubert, his rage played
Piano, when he drank I held him tight.

He gave all five of us some land and left.

I've copied him, stored his songbook
In my blood, invested his woods and money
In vengeance, in love poems after his death.

They are inhabited hard-handedly by strangers.
I am their son. I don't know his name.
He punched his name out of mine.

Scream

In how many rooms have I been a man here
In stockinged feet, scared that someone would see him
In the dressed sordidness of his birth.
'Wasn't it a shame to tear my flesh,
My boy, are you my umpteenth dead person too many?
But once you were there you could not be missed.'

But when he was there he could no longer reread
How high one can be in a woman's esteem.
She never wanted him. She loved him
The way one loves a pain that slowly passes.
Does he love her? It seems that her face
Still circulates in his when he sleeps.

Clean Sweep

I

Yesterday I became a wound nailed
To a stretcher and sang like a blue siren
Down the streets of this port city –
The ship lay ready to take me across.
My name, my poetry had forgotten me.

But like everyone I became an emergency,
A rare blood group in checked slippers,
A stumbling object of scorn
And piss, a mash of strips of cranial flesh
Raked together while I screamed, and sewing
Needles unbuttoned the coat of much pain.

I'd rather die than die
While I lived, lay alive recovering
Under the murderous look of white jailers.
They wrote their reports with my blood.

2

I was living wrong.
Time taught me all along
I didn't understand it
As you know, my time
Escaped from me in time
I'd lived an hour
And then expired –

A glow worm in a bubble

Never again found.
I lay by the machine
 I'm catheter-bound
In a darkness that gents
In aprons reported
Dazzlingly. I wasn't
Alive. A heart still fired.

Inspiration

No sir, I don't need a view, a vision
Or a visit from higher powers, no madam.
A summer morning, black coffee, cigarettes,
The singing example of a fly, a gnat
That attacks my absence with its drunken figures,
Such things suffice here to lift the skirts
Of a moist soul; to blind your critical eye
With her dumb crack, yes sir.

For me it's not about words, you see, but sentences
That come up the street from nowhere this morning
Like yawning children drunk from their sleep.
They play cautiously with each other's longings
And catch balls that no one throws over the hedges.
They lie fighting on the pavement hugging each other
And kiss at random their distant future.
It is those sentences that I find without meaning.

Tourist

I

Tattoos. Chip bags. Greasy quiffs laugh
And call to girls in the Handschoenmarkt.
They are necessary and significant
For without them this sun woudn't have the ghost of a chance.
Dented cola cans gleam like jewels,
Chains and buckles set stained-glass windows
Of the cathedral aflame again.
The praying vulgarity of that idling!
That calling to calves! Their laughter belongs!

Young flesh grows here in the street like grass on graves.

You wander through that false centre of your earnestness
And observe the map of all those clouds,
All those same, ever-changing clouds,
And can't find the town of your town.
You follow astonished the peaceful reality
Of your thoughts and don't move an inch.
With giant strides your motionless life rushes
Through centuries, barges its way to the Markt
And views that beating heart of historical fake.

2

Heat draws a membrane over the city's din.
You photograph the exhaustion of swelling trams,
The grey-twisted talk of walking beards
In Jodenstraat, the melting departure time
Of the trains, the stifling zoo that like a sea
Of stench washes over steamy Astridplein.

You've lived for thirty years in this bubble
Of brick above the Scheldt.
Here decades went walking without you
Like that endless water without an address.

Heat draws a membrane over the city's din.
Russian ships lie a stone's throw
From the Markt, rusting like your own life
In this steaming heat. Suddenly a tower bursts out
In ice crystals, a god weaves with his fists
A lacework of sounds. The membrane's ruptured.

Commitment

Unworldly, you say. But not of what world?
Outside the seething sun. And inside walking barefoot
Over the cool tiles of my floorless house, everything
Hangs in the air, a South, you, lots of money, me too,

Is that unworldly then? But not of what world?
So must I feed the stomach of my curiosity
With your misery? And do I not walk free in my dream?
Don't I have the right to sing when you suffer?

Or may my poetry not ask awkward questions
Of my poetry? Must I break my golden fingers
And read bloody gazettes with my powerless hands?
Must I interrupt my children's game for ever?

Must I weep at the news with grown-up eyes?
You have a great pain on the other side of the earth
Or here in my street, and I have mine, small, private
And unworldly, you say. But not of what world?

Crowning Glory

Death will come and it will have no one's
Eyes, Pavese,
And beneath my closed lids not a soul sleeps.
And what will go with me
Into my grave, is a few poems
Never written,
The crate of beer I drank before I left,
And China, China
That I've dreamt of here for a lifetime.

My death is the crown
On all the work I've not yet been able to do.
My death is the hat
On the brain I might have wanted.
My death is the time
That I would have liked to be while I was alive.
My death will come
And it will have everyone's eyes, Rilke,
Under my lids.

At a Grave

Got, from you, got
Two eyes to look at you,
My gaze never to see you again.

Got, from you, got
Two feet to visit you,
My itchy feet to leave you.

Got, from you, got
Two lips to kiss you,
A mouth never to speak to you again.

Got, from you, got
Two ears to hear you
Ask: who has disappeared?

Got, from you, got
Two hands to carry you
From there to the spot where I stand.

Got, from you, got me
To be here alone,
To be here together with you

Without you.

Inside and Outside

Trains. Hotels. Paris. The outside world!
What a word, I cannot abide it.
The world outside was the inside world
Of Le Chartier when we sat side by side
Over a Pinot Noir, my pig's innards
Grilled almost black, your golden liver
Venetian-style. We were more indigent then
And better looking, you prefer to leave
For longer and alone now, to see the outside world
That word! I cannot abide it.

You used to walk on my left
Into Florence and New York, and with my right
I wrote in the air another country.
Can I help it if it kept getting more real
And more vast in that shrinking head
Of this inside world? What a word,
I can't abide it, romanticism
And old-fashioned solism make me sick.
That alone we can travel together again.

Ex-Directory

A certain solitude's an odd construction.
One walks in one's memories through the tender door
Of a familiar address, the sun falls on its spot,
The bed's resplendent in the tall window at the front,
Your gaze lights us when you talk to me at night.

With growth and effort we've gone our own way

To sort our letters, to reread
The long distance we used to be good at.
Distance was an art we knew from close up
Then, no telephone knows what I mean.
Life daily forgets its own number.

The Bourgeois

But they're different people there, they have houses
In the South, double-barrelled names and wide terraces
With the prospect of an endless old age.
They lean back in their succulent gold
And have time squared from Swiss vaults.
I too write my cheques here, covered or not.

Oh, here or there, it's the same poetry
Of flesh that capitalises all its dreams.
It is the same prose of the bourgeois.
I too have mostly lived for myself, I too
Have gambled day and night, hoarded my days and nights.
But my secret savings book is everyone's.

The Shy One

You should have a good look at those people.
They come in with their shy feet
And sit hunched at table, small, invisible
Almost as if they hate their birth.
They eat with us out of politeness.

They drink our wine, their tongue loosens
And asks the questions no one wants to hear.
Our answer is the consoling biography
Of their absence. Their thinness smiles
At glasses and dishes, the candles illuminate
Their hard, unmade, narrow bed for later.

The Nameless Ones

A man, a woman, a couple, at some point came.
Not a soul around here knows their name.
I bump into their vague age daily
In Vinkenpark, they walk with gestures all round

Mumbling under their breath at the swans about.

They have caps on winter and summer, a bag
Of white sandwiches from childhood days
And blue wings they leave folded in one plane
And yellow papers – they don't read every page.

The Captain of the Kursk

No one can go top side.
I say this feeling my way.
I carve this in the iron
Of a wreck that's reeling away.

I've no God or cash for you
To ransom us with pounds.
My people are very few.
Our house has run aground.

We are locked up, are bound
In an outrageous plight
I have surrendered all
To water and salt, my birthright.

No one can go top side.
The stars hang there and fade
Jerkily, the streets
Of our villages go bad

In a vault full of cries
A rusting box of screams
That no one can hear top side.
No one can go top side.

We stay forever below.
We scratch our only support
In the sides, the leaky hull
Of a drunken wreck.

The Infinitive

To be yourself.
To be yourself no matter who.
But to be yourself.

To squander your right hand
On strangers, to translate your birthright
Into another, to train till you weep
In squinting at goals, to lose your head
in friends' worries,
But to be yourself.
To be yourself no matter who.
But to be yourself.

To buy your self-love
From peddlers, with your self-hatred
To train dogs, with your heart problem
To synchronise hundreds of clocks there
In a land overseas, in the middle
Of the night to bank electronically
As a snot-nose of seven, lost
In a vanished parental home.

To be yourself.
How splendid, how exhausting,
To be yourself no matter who.

The Drinker

I

Next to her pillow a breath
Of stink and drink in the dark.
God and Daddy, Mummy,
They've forgotten him! His mouth,
Dreaming aloud, seeks the breast.

She weeps, she swears, she whets
A knife on the rolling stone
Of his snores, she squeezes
Her cunt with fright, she knows
The whims of his prick.

And as, farting and cajoling,
He forces his way in, cursed
With long sweet names,
With slow thrusts and strokes,
She comes in disgust.

2

Morning. Resurrection. Grave smell.
Throw off the covers and get up.
No bread can assuage his hunger.
Pulling open a can trembling
And drinking, with short swigs, against
The cold and the retching, against
God and the alarm, against
The score of cigarette-ends from yesterday
In the washbasin, against
The smoke of today, the smell
Of morning, the smell of his wife
In all her absent forms.

Not daring to go in the shower
And anyway who's he washing for now.
Can't find his mug, her smile
In the mirror. Sitting
Jerking off naked on the edge of the bed
To clear his head, to get thirsty
Again for all that he loved,
Her alto, hoarse, their South
Invented on benches in parks,
Spring water deep in the rock.
Thirst thirst thirst.
The compelling morning prayer.

3
A long black hall
And at the end a bed.
Three times that night knocked
Out with love. His eyes
Bloodshot. His throat,
Wide open, drinks her gullet.

His eyes are glued to the ceiling.
Neon lights flick on and off, always
There's screaming somewhere, begging
For pills or injections, sobbing
In this long black hall.

In the morning a taxi home.
Would rather die over there
Than be bored with many.
And tomorrow to feel guilty
Because he hates those many so much,
All the drinkers and shooters and himself.

FROM I — Flesh in Uniform Is Fully Automatic

I

It's hard to say, hard
To work out when our journey began.
We face the umpteenth tunnel
And the cliff face is scribbled with thorn bushes.

One has left shattered in search of sleep,
Another laughs at his house that he saw on the way,
A third sucks on a harmonica in order to see his little son.
And we are all weighed down with rucksacks of photos
     and bread.

Someone over there sniggers that he doesn't exist,
But our whole group forms a close-knit unit of suckers.
Soon the train will come and take us to crystal stations.
We whistle silently on our knuckles.

It's hot. We're fleeing ahead of the army
And take out our anger on the plateaus and valleys,
The swelling sides of hills. But yonder people are walking
And our eyes set fire to their villages.

We walk through the train waiting for an arrival
And mumble hoarsely and incomprehensibly the name of
     our destination.
Most movements are too transparent to be true.
We entrust ourselves to the speed with which we disappeared

From our village, our town, it's difficult to say
If we left from necessity, love or boredom.
We all eat the same bread differently
And our slow life races ahead of us to stop us.

2

We sit bare-chested on the rocky bank
Sweating against the clock. Night brings no release
From the heat – the hottest summer of the century, they say.
In the distance, on the far bank of the invisible river
The headlights of the cars, the trains, the trams shine
And children left behind sleep fitfully in our thoughts
And devise together with their mothers our singing return.
But we, we look further than we can go over there.

Once, when we still studied the stories of the future
And lay joking and flirting like men together,
Once our dreams cast their strong nets
Across the water and built bridges of stone and text
Which competed hard with the high grace of seagulls.
Today we lean back unemployed in solidarity
Against a wall of heat. But our eyes go on pushing
Against that distance, in our languor that boy still stands
    straight.

When it becomes light we wash each other with piss and spit
And explore the road we have taken sitting down.
There must be an underground passage, a side-path, something
That today will save us from all that vastness.
We want clarity, the vague onward-speeding splendour
Of clouds and rivers is not enough for us, we want
A country with a mighty wall around it and bolted gates,
And that only we can go freely in and out of.

3

With gigantic pocket torches and whispers we scan,
Standing, bent or on our knees, the north side.
We never know if we are inside or outside the camp
And are not being pursued by anyone. That is the problem.

The woodland animals and we are jumbled together
In the same scream, we sometimes walk stinking scared.
No horizon yonder halves our brain like a dream
And the last map has evaporated from our blood.

For decades united by necessity, love, boredom,
We slowly put our shoulders under that leaden thought
Of salvation, force a door in the undergrowth
And see our reflections disappear among the trunks.

But we don't let go of them. Again we cast a mighty net
Of cries over the heads of our pedigree doubles.
And our cries for help glitter like a city under construction
Beneath the stars. Screaming intently is the art.

4

The tower stands there, at last, and we are dirty.
The square full of empty beer bottles, bread crusts
And other muck has been swept and shines, and those
who come after us can see themselves in it.

I patiently washed the face, the old breasts and feet
Of my wife and changed my underwear.
The tower stands there and the dwelling can begin,
    the sleeping
In this time of transition. (But what time is not one?)

We wearily raise the umpteenth glass
And hear the steps of the next shift pound.
And the same invisible songs that we sang down below
In the foundations, out there are clearly approaching.

They too, the workers of the nightshift, will come
To make fires with our tables, demolish our beds
And flatten our tower with iron ideas.
And in that pit of mud and mother's milk their mouths bloom.

But now the evening's still safe enough for parties.
Let us make love and talk and drink before they come, they,
The children with the brand-new flick knives and gold lighters,
The barbarians we made in a trice in the dark.

5
We enter the market where my parents live
And quicken our steps under the high arches
Of demolised arcades.

Armed ghosts have beaten us to it.
The kiosk lies like a a ball of music paper slung
Against the church porch.

The square is empty.

We plant in its heart a bunch of rifles
And lay our knives in a rose
Of rage on the stone.

A man strokes the cut dumbly and seeks
His thumb print,
His blood.

Rancour leaks from the hilt.
Hate licks his shoe.
We leave the square where my parents lived.

6
We are that century, that twentieth
Without number, I already said it
With the precision of a runaway tongue.

Don't take a photo of us.
Have compassion with a woman
Who doesn't know her sizes,
And don't shoot a film about paralysed men.

Don't make us men or into a story.
We are the naked ones who shroud themselves
In burning flags,
In the names of violated borders.

Our tailor has no material.
We pull our uniform of flesh
Over other people's bones to see ourselves.
We size each other up
With the measureless measure of God's absence.

Our educated accent is a mistake
Or a guess, and our axiom says:
We know nothing. We know nothing.
That's what we teach the children at school.

FROM III – We Were the Silent Ones after May 1945

9
We were few.
We were some.

We weren't just the job
For the left – it sang us no orientation.
We weren't grist to the mill
Of the right – they don't fret about edification.
We found between the selection
No golden mean or section.

We were a few.
We were others.

We were then neither mussel
Nor fish in the holy water font.
We were then neither red
Nor blue in a rainbow high
Tense with expectation.
We lived on your deprecation.

We were few.
We were some,

We lived by bread and Rimbaud
In ascetic bourgeois salons.
We drank the French kiss of soul pain black
Like Hadewijch.
We were your weak spot of hers.
There we found each other furtively.

10

We were few.
We were some.

We never bandaged our wounds in flags.
We didn't carry a banner, no nappy on sticks
Thrust proudly aloft, we ran like tears
Past all those broken families and streets.

We were lodge brothers without a lodge.
Our workplace sounded like a postponed kiss
And love became a university for two.
Not a soul taught light there.

Our pacifism bordered on hate
And poetry was propaganda for deaf ears.
We became a cryptic sob in the throat
Of Mondrian, his brush did not bat an eyelid.

We were squarely against his square
Squared, we remained blind
To his primary palette, we remained deaf
To squarely turning boogie-woogies.

We were a few.
We were others.

11

Field preachers got high on hammers
And sickles and jerked us off with their mounths.
And dockers sang themselves hoarse in the throttling weepie
Of a world-embracing pair of hands.
Priests cursed the church for the shop floor
And they too worked the conveyor belt.

We were the cowards. We only later saw the daring
Of our lonely gangway, no Trotsky can airbrush us out
In the sordid deceit of international scrums.
Only our grieving bodies had the impact
Of life-like slogans. We were silent rhetorically.
We had no power but the force of our inaction.

We formed a mass confluence of absent ones
On the public platform. We never signed
Another's manifestos, we hid
Our singular signal under a bushel.
We measured our future with the daily suicide
Of Chamfort and Jos de Haes, we reached out to each other

Across the graves of our children's children.
We studied the busy pride of boredom
And swore by a conspiracy of the aloof.
We would not be pacified, would not be screwed
By a deluge of smart shit, we stayed as penniless
As these poems, letters scattered like ashes.

13
We curled up dejectedly in the spare wheel
Of the wagon of May sixty-eight.

We slept on our feet,
We liked to predict ourselves.
We dreamt upright
And drew transparent bills on each other.
We lived vertically
And our feet sought a point of attachment
In the thread of older traditions.

We missed our stolid Latin when we mourned.
We were fatally ill, in search of a deathbed.
In others' eyes we lived and partied.
On blood money in the world bank of Golgotha.
We were criminals without records.
Our crime was we'd as yet done no wrong.
We did not act.
We lived in our thoughts
And thought we were living.

We rewrote Athens, Schubert and Rembrandt
In the tongue of our vanished home region.
We wrote theses on our personal pathos.
We gave our heart a degree.
We gained doctorates in lyricism.
We set our sights on many forward positions
Without status. We couldn't find our feet.

Ours heads spun like a dancing dervish caged
In the head of a dancing dervish.
We called for each other. We called to any other.
We walked round each other in wide arcs dancing
With caution, we were explosives then.

14
We were few.
We were some.
We were others.

We never touched up the Christian lap
Of trade unions, never bumbled democratically
On wings of high fliers to the top of the party –
We played with fire in their sleep.
We became black sheep in cloned pens

Full of baby boomers, we descended like white ravens
On a cage full of postmodern parrots.

We clung to each other.
We clung to each other like loose sand,
A widespread street gang of daydreamers,
A hermetic clique of hermits.
We lived on our knees
And worshipped the sun of not knowing
And kissed the eternal light of scepsis.
Nowhere were we central.

We were poor and speculated on the exchange
Of intellectual tradition.
We acted with prior inside knowledge
From forgotten ages.
We became heroes to our precursors.
We were jeered at by our successors.
We became, dead earnest, our own laughing stock.

We were the open wound
Of a closed book.
We were the closed mouth
Of an open question.

16
I'll write we by your leave a bit longer,
I can't say otherwise.
We were not simply born after May forty-five.
We were not simply born.
We were not simply.
We were simply not.

We played a pioneering role in a mouth without man.
We got all worked up in a tongue with no mouth.
We circulated like viruses all over the screen.
The word made flesh became an open secret
Behind the bolts and bars of any tabernacles.
We hanged ourselves in poems deprived of their poet.

We were not simple. We simply were not.
We had no close family, and so were related.
We did not swim about in a letter by Darwin.
We do not pluck a heart from the heart of a stone
Rolled uphill by my father.
We did not roll out of a mother, a template for life.

We had no mirrors at home
And let our image wander in papers and pubs.
We become rabble for the local committee,
Bohemian lyrics and dirt from the street.
There we bought our documents back from ourselves.
Many phrases together produced no emotion.

I'll write we by your leave a bit longer,
I can't put it differently.
We were the silent ones after May forty-five.
We were the silent ones of May sixty-eight.
We were not simple.
We simply were not.

19
We were few.

We found in the belittling bombast of bosses
No trace of you, no spark of me,
No whiff of erotic rhetoric,

No intimate story and no inner fact.
The raw sex of emotion for leaders was a thorn
In the flesh of the class struggle.

We were some.

We spoke to each other like wildfire
In the distance. We frequented ourselves
Like burning secrets, we were not friends
With each other nor could we be friends with me.
We must not disentangle the dream we had
Of you from ourselves.

We were a few.

And all that was useful was the exclusive rhythm
Of cursing under the breath, the fleshy vision
That slept in the paintbrush of Bosch, the tautly
Strung string in a grand of Igor Stravinsky's.
All that was useful was your stuttering reading
That letter by letter completes what I write.

We were others.

20
We were few.
We, uniquely, had dropped our village
From the height of our pretension.
We gravitated from the squalid provinces
To garishly filmed handholds of centres.
We were left unique, unanimous and universal behind

In the hall.
We were some.

We were lived for all we were worth.
There was no loop around our minds.
There was no give in our loose-living ways.
Nowhere were we central.

We were a few.
We had not of ourselves a self-evident content
Of you and me, it was hard to hold
Ourselves dear, we did not hold on to ourselves.
We held ourselves in contempt.
We could not hold out.

We were others.
Our individual was on fire like the diary
Of a terrorist lost in the desert.
In its living room our nationalism shifted
To the right and read papers rewritten
with boiling eyes.

We were few. Some. A few. Others.
Artists specialised
In disappearance, poets became empirical scientists
Of whiteness, and no one had a word to say.
No one had anything to say but no one.
Politicians voted us out.

FROM IV — How Does My City Look When I Dream It?

3
An ambitious young man has practically no imagination
To look further than his imagination.

I was twenty-one and famous in the family,
My hopscotch squares were written in the stars.

I was twenty-one and decried in the milieu
Of my world-wide pretensions.

My local future flew round my neck
Like a rampart of dreams with no gate.

A siren call like Antwerp in those years gained its status
Of hard reality.

It marching orders were in my eyes meant personally
Like a smart train, a supersonic back way

To a harbour where one moors to live and work
On a drunken ship, I knew my Rimbaud.

Such a super-strong verb as Antwerp rang in my ears
Like a city based on pure astonishment.

Initiailly I didn't have the heart, the money
To take my freedom to heart, to make it pay.

Sometimes someone must wait until the rug
In the boy's room catches fire beneath his feet.

A house full of the dead finally pointed me to the burning
Doorway, my deserted birthplace ran fast

And blazing, winding and roaring after me
And took me to the station.

4
The whole street hung out of the windows
Like the day when I soon comprehend my birth.

No hand, no kiss, no nod put me on the train
There , the running board scorched sole and soul.

I stumbled for years through the compartments, angry
And shaken up I slowly wrote this down.

For whom? I'd not the remotest idea.
I still say, I've not the remotest idea about us.

Yet at night we are the first I meet
Tonight, we wear are masks from home in bed.

I sleep badly here anyway, I can't find my feet
In your feet, my dreams keep me awake.

My nights are three sisters below with pale faces
Singing in the scorched kitchen.

They wave laughing to my brother as large as life again
On his wrecked bike.
I am the last one I saw over there perhaps,
Every landscape leaves us in uncertainty.

I had to quickly do all kinds of things, bury my father
With your gestures, consoling my mother

In her own dialect that we've no way of knowing.
We dub her open secret.

She's now on her way to us. But tomorrow, tomorrow
We'll be hers. Here's. Each other's.

5
Sooner
Or later, Baghdad
Or Berchem, rain
Or shine, nonsense
Or Nolens, war
Or peace,

In the mornings I always sit embarrassed with my big mouth
In your smallest room and gape at us.
And in the afternoons I always lie with my bike
In our grass on our Scheldt and count my ships.
Their booming shadows stroke my son's flat
Over there in the green of Gerlachekaai.

But I'm never from here,
I have no street plan in my pocket of our relationship.

And I am never yours,
One uses first names to reveal dryly and briefly
Other people's tears.

And I am never ours,
Like most people I lead a different life from you.

I still hear my arrival, the Keyserlei sounded
Like a nagging sore, a birth
Silently shot to shreds.

Days, months, years in the evenings I slump
Shifting back and forth in your empty chair.

And at night in your comfortable bars
And beds I move here at the highest level
Of my impotence, I find myself here
At the lowest level of your species.

I look for my passport, it lies open
And bare in the filthy cradle of your stream.
And its photo is fading.

7
It's a Friday night in August and hot.
My wife lies naked and legs apart asleep
In front of the screen in the hectic rhythm
Of commercials, marching child soldiers
And the last 32 in Driekoningenstraat.
Here in front of me, on the blue-and-yellow check tablecloth
A bottle of fizzy water, two empty glasses and a tray.

Beneath my pen this little still life becomes a human being
Turned into a plane, a clammy
Stain, a dark
Spot.

And nothing but this black matter enlightens my presence.

Each of these letters is the mortal remains
Of my two hundred bones and countless dead over there
In Uganda.
My face feels timeless
Like every product of my time.

My wife is caught up naked and asleep
In the rocking talk of the Turkish neighbours, the dull cadence
Of tramping child soldiers, the craven metre
Of a man writing in the style of the petty thief.

Just yesterday I saw my boy's room and the street
Below as a serious interplay,
A musical challenge
Of billions of mouths, a gigantic soul
In the making,
Yes,
Soul.

Its etymology is unknown.
But I was only just ten
And my soul was the shape of my body.

from V — It Is a Splendid Book

I

It is a splendid book.
It comes from my father and mother
And gets lost here, it runs
Far ahead of me with my sons.

It is a splendid book
In its earliest dawn embroidered
With future facts, flecked
With hundreds of clicking tongues.

It is a splendid book.
It pounds with monkey blood
And angels' talk, it smells
Of unexploited springs.

Interviews

1

You ask about my vision after forty years'writing, my vision!
Are you insulting me or my poetry?
I was still young, a child, and sat at this table
To make room for what I don't know.

My instinct's blind groping by an elderly man with no prospect
Except this landscape, a garden wall built of brick.
And high above the lazy trail of a jet fighter, still
As a line of coke, and a screeching cloud

Of seagulls, and nothing else but blue blue blue the sky,
The sun's copper extinguishing bin.
As always, I can't be compared to anything
In this room, how can I exist?

Too often, too long, too thoroughly I've sat here in the dark
Looking at the light, too long
I've fixed the golden pupil in the sun's paternal eye
To look deeper, further than me.

2

What moves someone,
The slow life's work of a miniature
On ivory, to educate a small class
In Latin,

What moves someone,
To train a dog, a falcon
For hunting, the miracle
Of a diamond wedding,

What moves someone,
That's not the stuff of small talk, no
That doesn't make for good chitchat,
That isn't fit fodder for papers or mikes.

What moves someone is the prim pretension
Of glands and knowledge,
A pride that kneels before the mirror
Of tradition.

One slowly learns how to dash off a haiku
By reading Parmenides
And so being cured of this garrulous time,
Its misunderstood democracy.

This afternoon I hear Marcus Aurelius again.
He says in his private notes:
'Socrates called the opinions of the majority
Horror stories, fit to frighten children with.'

I

Tell the children we're no good.
Tell them that we make children at night
And next morning benignly trash them, tell
The son who plays up at table and sings,
Appeasing hunger with ditties, tell him

That we'll empty his mouth of the music,

That we'll drag him down with milk
And thrashings, hard-earned bread and exams.
Tell him his thirst will have to learn manners
From us pygmies, the fathers and mothers.
We call the tune, but make few demands.

2

Tell the children we're no good.
Tell the daughter who twirls in her sleep
That a dreamt waltz isn't a job, tell her
The giddy flourish of three-four time
Will cripple her feet. We taught her to walk once,

To live our life slowly, proceeding with caution.

We have no time to waste on dancing:
And we worship instead God's law of the clock,
The zone of reality that's navigable.
We must spare our loved one the pain
Of swans enmeshed in a lake of tutus.

3

Tell the children we're no good.
They must pay for the dung pit, the cesspool
That we dug in our bank of clouds, they must
Clear out the heavenly sewers, that dump filled
With shit in azure the Ancients sang of.

My primal sin has eclipsed all their suns.

Our light was bountiful once. We left it
Polluted, there isn't a star
To be seen in the streets, we're being electrically
Dazzled. Our minds jumped over the moon.
And the prospect of death sometimes seems a relief.

Jealous

A stranger went through and crossed out all my letters to us
And accuses me of tics and feigned inspiration. Here.
I have no defence. You too think your mirrors have gone
Haywire when you see me get drunk, going over the edge,
Flipped by your images worked up in my muzzy head.

They must, I know, cure me, they must be removed
And perhaps I don't make them for you, since someone else
    looks over my shoulder.
And perhaps I don't make them for us, I'm making you public.
And they must be smashed, they must perish perhaps,
My desire for you has long since exceeded our couple here.

A third party went through, deleted all my letters to us.
Yet I dare to continue confessing, that indecency
Of heart's secrets that poison love with love,
Listen. Question me. I'll confess everything,
I'm crazy about all that's yours and jealous, jealous

Of your old, snow-white dancing girl's feet
That sleepless, at night, in the hottest depth of the the summer
Come blossoming downstairs, I hold them here step
By step in my hand to forget my own ungainly
Gait, I'd like to be snowy and quick as you,

Jealous of your tact, your dislike of confessions
All over the carpet, wordy sex and family coats-of-arms,
Jealous of that wonderful talent of your hatred of men
Who hoist women onto pedestals and lyrically jealous
Of your sober reading glasses, they see us, even without poems,

Jealous of your tears of loyalty to that left-wing party stuff
Of beefsteak and Bach, of that clinical, cynical smile
With which your alert butterflies of fingers sweep old money
Off the table, I jingle onto the floor of home
Back then, jealous of your today, your dislike of nostalgia.

Bombast

We've all gone post
And neo these days!
Your declarations of love?
Postmortal piffle

Of adolescents!

Creations? Cremations
Of neoprosodic patients
In sackcloth and ashes!
Astmatic exclamation marks?

Bombast!

Cliché

Leave her alone.
And leave her alone all day long.
And wait, undergo
The dragging clock of her siren call.

Don't change tack.

Wait.
And in the evening find
The door and knock and embrace
The exciting drudgery
Of your love. Keep to yourself the cliché

That our parting is kissing its way to us.

Translator's Note

THE ANTWERP-BASED poet Leonard Nolens (born in 1947), who studied modern languages and subsequently worked as a freelance translator, once claimed to be more interested in his 'poetic identity' than in biographical details like those just given. Ideally, he argued, his curriculum vitae would consist solely of his name and the thousand or so poems last collected in 2011 as *Manieren van leven* (Ways of Life). However, while his poetic activity remains central, any suggestion that we are dealing with an unworldly recluse is dispelled by the sparkle of his voluminous *Dagboek van een dichter* (Poet's Diary, 2009), where engagement with people, art, ideas and the world around him are evident on every page.

Moreover, he writes with full awareness of the linguistic and cultural politics of his native land. The poem 'Place and Date' from the cycle 'The Enduring Departure' begins with the much-quoted lines:

> I was born in Belgium, I'm Belgian.
> But Belgium was never born in me.

It looks at first sight as if we are being confronted with a familiar topos: the widespread disillusion of Dutch-speaking Belgians or Flemings with their precarious constitutional monarchy. But the concept of 'Flanders' does not define him completely either; it is at best 'a modern artificial mother'. His own earliest roots lie in the province of Limburg and its dialect ('the heart-breaking gabble I study'), positioning him on the margins of Dutch-language poetry in Belgium. This may seem like affectation or even reverse hubris, but such marginalism offers a fruitful perspective. The poet's sensibility is defined as follows:

> My reality has lots of knowledge
> Of things that escape it daily.
> Absence is its most natural heart.
>   ('Slave Girl')

Nolens' earliest work, from the collection *Twee vormen van zwijgen* (Two Forms of Silence, 1975) to *Alle tijd van de wereld* (All the Time in the World, 1979) , is an attempt, mostly vain, to understand and relate to himself and others through poetry. The poetry specialist Hugo Brems describes what he sees as the core paradox underlying this early work: '… the poetic word demolishes reality, severs all pre-established links with his fellow-men, but at the same time it strives to be a means of making reality and of establishing contact with others.' Unsurprisingly, this phase in his development has been characterised as 'tortured' and 'tormented'. The poetry is also haunted by the presence of such giants of twentieth-century European lyricism as Rilke, Valéry, Neruda, Mandelstam, Pavese and Celan, with whom he has arguably more affinity than with much poetry from the Dutch-language canon.

Facile pathos is eschewed:

> I've no powerful feeling for life, chest puffed out.
> I've no splendid emotional life to lavish
> Or sick spots which are supposed to make myself more popular
> With weepy people and the public purse.
>   ('Undercurrent')

Life is seen bleakly as 'a delivery room with no door'. The poems are presented unapologetically, comments the critic Rob Schouten, as 'expressions of spiritual states', to which the reader is free to respond or not.

From the mid-1980s on tone and form become more sober, the imagery more classical:

> She sleeps and all is still. Then it snows in the rooms
> > Of the house which I inhabit with my lover.
> > ('Tributary')

The volume of love poetry mounts, and it becomes his best-selling genre. In it an urgent eroticism is interwoven with the critical affirmation of an enduring relationship. A few samples:

> We sit naked at table. Your eyes light up the room.
> > ('Verklärte Nacht')

> You slept in your name till I came and said it.
> > ('L*')

> I jerk her face towards me
> And lick and swallow all her tears.
> > ('Craw')

> My blond light-hearted one hurries half-naked
> And fused with her swirling skirt
> Through the room.
> > ('Alice')

> Keep to yourself the cliché
> That our parting is kissing its way to us.
> > ('Cliché')

With the long cycle *Bres* (Breach, 2007), ten years in the writing, the poetry abandons the restrictive 'I' for 'we' in a (partial) portrait of his generation, with its passions and compromises:

> We curled up dejectedly in the spare wheel
> Of the wagon of May sixty-eight.

In this cycle, whose Dutch title has the same (ironic) associations of collective military endeavour, commitment and sacrifice as its English equivalent, but can also be read as referring to a disastrous loss, Nolens reaches new, hypnotic rhetorical heights.

> We were few.
> We were some.
>
> We never bandaged our wounds in flags.
> We didn't carry a banner, no nappy on sticks
> Thrust proudly aloft, we ran like tears
> Past all those broken families and streets.
>
> We were lodge brothers without a lodge.
> Our workplace sounded like a postponed kiss
> And love became a university for two.
> Not a soul taught light there.

In *Zeg aan de kinderen dat wij niet deugen* (Tell the Children We're No Good, 2011) Nolens evokes another collective, that of guilty parents:

> Tell the children we're no good.
> Tell the daughter who twirls in her sleep
> That a dreamt waltz isn't a job, tell her

The giddy flourish of three-four time
Will cripple her feet. We taught her to walk once,

To live our life slowly, proceeding with caution.

We have no time to waste on dancing:
And we worship instead God's law of the clock,
The zone of reality that's navigable.
We must spare our loved one the pain
Of swans enmeshed in a lake of tutus.

A marked feature of the later verse, and specifically *Bres*, is its regular, often almost incantatory repetition. Rhythmically lines are often constructed of a regular number of pulses and with sophisticated use of assonance. Full rhymes are very much the exception.

Throughout his prolific career Nolens has plumbed the Dutch language for its resonances, rich associations and ambiguities, and has achieved a powerful musicality. In a recent interview, given on the occasion of the award of the prestigious Prize for Dutch Literature in 2012, the poet set out succinctly his optimum requirements for a poem. It must be at once musical, communicating with the reader's 'listening eye', plastic, narrative and reflective. A tall order, but one which Leonard Nolens' best poems fulfil triumphantly.